Acts of Kindness

A Collaborative Work Among Many Authors

ISBN: 978-1-989506-24-0

DEDICATION

To those who make the world a better place by their selfless acts of kindness.

ACKNOWLEDGMENTS

I'd like to acknowledge and thank every person who made this book possible. Thank you to the authors who shared their stories, thank you to Alex Goubar for the cover art, thank you to my team at Pandamonium Publishing House, and thank you to our readers who make our work possible.

Thank you to the millions of people around the world who make a difference in the lives of others with their acts of kindness, empathy, respect, and optimism.

Thank you to all of those who read this book, pass it along, and find inspiration in the pages.

"MY WISH FOR YOU IS THAT YOU CONTINUE. CONTINUE TO BE WHO YOU ARE, TO ASTONISH A MEAN WORLD WITH YOUR ACTS OF KINDNESS."
-MAYA ANGELOU

1
A RANDOM ACT OF KINDNESS
BY S.P. TAYLOR

One random act of kindness is all it takes to literally change a life. My story is about how someone's good deed made a difference in mine and my children's lives. How one person's generosity was a gift that gave us hope and started us on a wonderful new journey.

One act of kindness can change a life. I always knew this and believed in the magic of being kind. My mom once said I was *"too kind for this world"* but I wasn't offended as I feigned to be. I was secretly overjoyed that someone noticed my kindness. I made an impact and that made me proud. Life has made it such that I have endured great happiness and much sadness. Like poppies and daisies together in a beautiful bouquet, better yet, a garden. The saddest and the happiest of flowers (or so I always thought) both together sharing a space in time.

"Never give up," I would tell my boys when they

were little men. Keep moving one foot in front of the other.

I tried very hard to be the example so that they would see that no matter what happens to you, only you will decide how it will affect you.

Once my eldest asked, "Why were you nice to her, mom? She was mean!"

"Perhaps she had a bad day," I responded, "and besides, I am not mean." I teased.

The pout on his face and his crinkly brow were an indication that he wasn't quite there yet. His understanding of the power one holds when being kind not fully developed.

"You're too nice mom," the middle child once said, "it makes me so mad."

He was always seeking justice. Why be kind if someone doesn't deserve it? If someone is making your life harder? And so, the lessons began with each step we took as the boys grew, in our small world.

A little light of hope happened upon us one summer. After much thought and looking, I found the one! The house that would be ours. Years of striving for this goal had passed. Some days my thoughts filled with the idea that it would never happen, yet here it was. That feeling of knowing and that chance I wanted to take.

I knew putting in an offer meant full price as the markets were high and homes in my price range going fast. I offered all I could, the asking price. I couldn't budge a cent higher and I was warned there would be an over bid. I took a chance because something told me too. Perhaps it was the house itself. Some say that houses take on the personality of the ones who've lived there. Like a sponge, the energy seeps into every facet of the home. This house had love. And I wanted so very badly for it to be ours.

"Should I write a letter?" I joked with my realtor.

"It can't hurt," was her reply. And so, I started writing.

Dear Homeowners, I am a single mom and I come in a pack with three great boys. I had the pleasure of viewing your lovely home and liked it so much I took a chance and gave you an offer! I am not certain if many people write letters anymore, but I thought to perhaps give it a try so that you would know a bit about me and my family in hopes you would consider us. I have spent the last six years working very hard to move ahead so that the boys and I can have a good life. I have had a few bumpy rides but after a lot of grit and determination I am ready now to enjoy the next journey of owning my own home. I currently rent a small bungalow (top floor only) and have been there for five years. It is too small for us as my boys are growing into men and I look forward to giving them an opportunity to have some space for themselves. My boys are great, and I just know they will enjoy and love your home. The neighbourhood is perfect as my middle one attends high school around the corner. And my youngest will be joining him next year. My oldest son uses a cane to walk, so the extra support you have within your bathrooms will prove most useful for him and was a great asset when I saw them. My sister lives in the neighbourhood as well. We are both very close and I would love the opportunity for our boys to continue to grow up together. I love gardens. Yours is lovely! I find solace and peace when I work with plants. Gardening really is the only time my mind will stop thinking. My thumb is not quite green, but I hope it will be one day. Thanks for taking the time to read this letter and looking at my offer. I think you have a great home and would love the opportunity to purchase it from you. Kind regards, A Loving Mom.

Three offers went in. Mine was the lowest. I stayed steady and determined and I prayed. A part of me felt, in my even trying, that that was good enough. I was courageous enough to take the chance and this was what really mattered. The other part wanted so badly for the owner of the home to see me, to hear my story, to give me a chance. I will never know how much she lost accepting my offer. But with her sacrifice she gave me my dream, a house for my boys. One that was *ours*. We didn't have to share it. We could be ourselves in our own space with the joy in knowing the house was fully and completely our own. A home!

Her kindness changed me. I am not sure how or when, but one day I will pay this one act of kindness forward. In the meantime, I will keep putting one foot in front of the other spreading a little kindness along the way. The owner gave more than a home for the boys and me; her kindness taught them a valuable lesson. Her kindness gave them hope and let them believe. It was her kindness that made them understand what mom was saying all along. Be kind, spread it all around every aspect of your life and one day, life may just surprise you.

2
FINDING KINDNESS IN AN OVERGROWN LAWN
BY MARY HASSELL

During my husband's final illness, I spent almost every day in the hospital at his bedside. Although I did nothing physical during those hours except for walking the halls, adjusting his bedding, and holding a straw to his mouth so he could sip water, I went home exhausted every night and would collapse into a chair. Often, I fell asleep sitting up in the clothes I had worn during the day.

One night a gentle knock and a muffled growl from my dog brought me to consciousness. I stood up stiffly. The laundry I had been folding when I fell asleep fell to my feet. I opened the door to a pajama clad woman. It was Josie. I worked with her and she had become my unofficial liaison with the rest of the staff and the administration during my emergency leave.

"I won't come in." she said. "I don't want to disturb you, but I thought you might enjoy something from Tim

Hortons," She handed me large paper cup of herbal tea and a bag containing a sandwich and a donut.

Despite the untidy state of my house I invited her inside. She ignored the dishes in the sink and the forgotten cups on the coffee table and took a seat on the couch next to the laundry. I ate the sandwich and the donut, tasting neither, while she chatted about my students and what was going on at school. She assured me that the substitute teacher was skilled and caring.

When I finished eating, I walked Josie to the front step. I noticed she was looking at my large, neglected, overgrown lawn filled with dozens of dandelions and other weeds.

"I don't have the energy to even think about mowing it," I said as we hugged goodbye.

The next day when Josie called, I tried repeatedly to refuse her offer of help with the lawn. Her plan, already set into motion, was to have my teaching colleagues work on the yard. It seemed too overwhelming to contemplate and much too much to accept.

"Please let us help you," she begged. "We all care about you and this is one way we can demonstrate how much. Please. Please let us do this."

And so, I was bullied into this act of kindness.

"You don't even have to be there. You can stay at the hospital with Gary," she said.

On the appointed day I left the hospital earlier than usual so I could thank them. The nurse promised she would call if there was the slightest change. I had become familiar with the nursing staff in the few weeks I had been coming and they were stationed just a few feet from Gary's bed in ICU, so I felt comfortable leaving.

As I turned the corner onto my street, I saw them - a dozen men and women all shapes and sizes wearing gardening clothes and straw hats. They were working hard, some on their knees in the flower beds, and some pushing lawn mowers. In the few seconds it took to drive up the street I could see them laughing and joking with each other as they worked on the yard just the way they did in the staff room at school

I had to park on the street. Two pickups and an SUV were in my usual spot on the driveway. I slammed the car door and walked toward the people I had taught with for nearly a decade.

Everyone stopped for a moment and looked towards me. I found it difficult to talk. My words choked me. I was barely able to say thanks. Josie squeezed my hand and enveloped me in a comforting embrace.

"We're almost finished and then we'll leave. Your grass is done and most of the dandelion are gone too."

My gratitude was mixed with shame. Shame at the state of my house and yard. Shame that I needed help. And shame that I had to be bullied into accepting help from people who cared.

My inadequate mumblings of gratitude were interrupted with the principal's arrival. A few of the teachers ripped off their grass-stained gardening gloves and helped her carry pizza and beer over to the group. We ate together picnic style on the grass, comfortable with each other and happy to be together.

The chocolate covered strawberries and pastries I sent to the staff room the next day didn't come close to expressing my gratitude for their love and compassion on that day and on the many sad days to follow.

3
BEST FRIENDS
BY JAKE EVANOF

They say that as we get older, we discover who our true friends are. The ones that can make you laugh so hard you cry, the ones that really understand who you are as a person and the ones that are always there by your side no matter what.

Well, I feel like I've always known who my best friends were, but this story is about one of those times where I really knew for sure. It was back towards the end of high school and everyone was really excited! We were all graduating soon and a whole new chapter of our lives was about to unfold. *Were you going to University? College? Straight to work?* This was the catalyst to most conversations.

So, what was my plan for the fall? Well, that was the kicker; I had recently discovered that in order to get into my dream program, I would have to go back for a fifth year of high school to upgrade some of my credits. It wasn't going to be ideal, but I couldn't let this one setback hinder the pursuit to follow my passion. That summer went about the same as any other; Campfires, Video Games and Adventures, but like all great things, it had to come to an end.

Come September I was having a particularly tough time because as most of my close friends were getting ready to begin their new journeys, I guess I felt stuck. Two of my best friends saw this and they came up with a plan.

It was September 17th, 2011, the day of my birthday. I received a phone call in the early afternoon; Mitch and Harrison were on the other end. They told me they had a surprise for me and that I should come outside, so I did. I was met by both of them and a mysterious envelope on my front porch. I opened it up and lo and behold, it contained a riddle that would launch an incredibly nostalgic scavenger hunt.

The clever clues would end up leading us all throughout different landmarks in Hamilton that were significant to our friendship. The day began at our old elementary school and from there brought us to stops at our favorite Future Shop, a local Kelsey's that we frequented and even the flower shop that I got my prom dates corsage from.

Finally, we ended up in the treehouse in my backyard where they unveiled a surprise gag gift that they obtained from a local adult entertainment shop. I loved that day, not only because I got to go on one last summer adventure with my buddies, down memory lane no less…

but really because they didn't have to do any of that for me and it showed just how much they truly care. So, if you guys ever end up reading this, I just wanted to say thank you. You're my best friends and nothing is ever going to change that.

4

DOG GONE'IT
BY M.L. MAPLE

I'm often surprised about how much people can care for strangers. An early Tuesday morning last summer proved this. I was walking my golden retriever, Stan, like I usually did near a path by my house. We had walked this particular path each day during the week from Monday to Friday and we nicely settled into a routine over the years. Stan was getting old and so was I if I'm being honest. Well into my eighties, it was now just me and my dog.

We enjoyed the usual sights and sounds and said hello to all the familiar faces. As we were wrapping up our morning, there was a noise in the bushes to the left of us. I stopped dead in my tracks as my vision settled on the creature; it was a coyote, in the daylight no less. I was frozen in fear, I didn't know if it was rabid or if it would attack Stan or even me! There was no way that either of us could fight it off.

Suddenly, as the coyote continued to stare us down, there

was another sound; someone was hitting the ground with a stick, waving their hands, and yelling. I dared not turn around just incase the coyote made his move.

The animal turned away from us and started running back to the bushes where he'd come from. I breathed a huge sigh of relief and faced the stranger.

"Thank you so much for scaring him off, I wasn't sure what was about to happen, but I'm grateful you were here to help!" I said.

"I can imagine how scared you were," the gentleman said. "The good news is, that the coyote is a resident here, he's got a pretty bad limp for whatever reason, but he's not been known to attack people or dogs."

"Well, thanks again for helping us. Stan and I weren't sure what was going to happen, but you saved the day."

"I'm glad to be of help. I'm a huge animal lover and I've let the wildlife people here in the city know about the coyote. Hopefully, they can rehome him in a nice forest somewhere and get him some help for that leg," he said.

"That would be good, I certainly hope so," I said with a smile. "Thank you again for being at the right place at the right time."

"I'm happy to be of service. My dog, looked just like yours…lost him last summer to cancer. I'm not sure if I'm ready for another one just quite yet," he said quietly.

"I understand how hard it is to lose a pet, it's like losing a family member. I'm so sorry for your loss," I said. "If you'd ever like to walk Stan or spend some time with him, I'd be happy to extend that invitation to you. Maybe it will help you through the grieving process."

"Thank you, that's very kind," the man said as he knelt to pat Stan on the head. "I may take you up on that."

5

INSPIRATIONAL ALLIANCE
BY DELL GABLE

The repetitive thumping emanating from the end of the conference table, blended with the thought-provoking verbal bombardment, awakening the mundane listless ambience of the board room.

Observing the unquestionable impulse to chronicle every spoken word, hammered out with meticulous precision on the Braille typewriter - awakened my inner self. Participating in a world I was unaccustomed to, over a period of several months and becoming acquainted with all the folks; we shared stories and adventures in our lives. Relationships were forged, conversation ebbed and flowed. A lighthearted nonchalant tempo filled the air. It was the monthly gathering of vision loss and non-sighted folks.

"We strongly object to the term Blind, and the unnecessary connotation implying weakness, deficiency."

They were motivated with the desire to be recognized, indistinguishable from others in an equal, nonprejudicial way. There was a determined, goal setting mindset of those in attendance. A gentleman, who sat at the table, spoke enthusiastically about his recent trip overseas. Details of each specific country that he and his companion had visited, entertained, and amused everyone; Belgium, France, Spain, and England, shared the spotlight. Differentiating between cultures, highlighting subtle nuances, his story fascinated me. I was astounded.

The three-week vacation overseas reinforced belief in himself. He declared a refreshed outlook, because of travelling to Europe.

Occasionally the thump of the Braille machine, a marvel of technology, would abruptly stop. Unabated, conversation would continue. Television programs were a frequent topic, movies, the latest newsworthy events.

Anxious to express herself, Susan abruptly spoke up, amusing everyone with the latest pop culture news, reflecting upon a period in her life when she and a few of her sighted friends travelled to California in a reconditioned school bus.

"My friends, loyal to my needs, gave me the courage to say yes, I would love to travel with you, under one condition, I wasn't going to be a burden, extra cargo, a nuisance. My parents were very supportive, they trusted my girlfriends', one hundred percent. I was full of uncertainty, I was young at the time, unaware of a lot of things," she said, with conviction.

Having suffered a debilitating accident, rendering him blind, Louis Braille 1809 -1852 was determined to overcome his tragic loss of eyesight. He forged ahead and developed a remarkable coding system. Keys were manually manipulated with one's fingers, which in turn would produce configured embossed dots interpreted as the alphabet. Today, with the use of computer technology software, computer monitors allow the vision impaired to read text. Speech synthesis software creates an artificial production of human speech, enabling users to turn text into speech.

A skilled, small engine mechanic, seated at the table, recalled a challenging gas-powered lawnmower repair, that he had encountered. Timelines were not an issue. With assistance, he was able to reconstruct the internal combustion lawnmower engine on schedule.

Without hesitation, attendees would generously acknowledge those who willingly shared their experiences. Their congenial mood fostered a verbally rich environment.

"I was involved in a workplace accident," an attendee spoke candidly, calmly expressing himself before the receptive group, "a highly flammable container of combustible material ignited while I was servicing its holding tank and I was thrown backwards several feet, collapsing on the shop floor. I don't remember a thing, of course, I woke up in the hospital, my immediate reaction was fear and disbelief."

He was told that he had permanently lost his eyesight. He had survived a catastrophic accident. Months of rehabilitation would enable him to properly function again in a reasonable manner. A companion dog was immediately dispatched. Months of training and bonding, along with several modifications to his living accommodations proved to be a success.

I enjoyed participating in the monthly sessions, offering my services, reading newspapers, magazines to groups of folks on a casual, personal level in their homes. The bond of friendship is special. My motives were never evaluated in a disrespectful manner. It was clear from the beginning that my intentions were in good faith. I was prepared to be objective and benefit wholeheartedly.

A casual acquaintance shared some regretful news, her brother had been involved in a very serious auto accident, resulting in permanent loss of sight. Would I be willing to voice record a few of his textbooks? She wondered. This would enable him to pursue the complex process of adapting to the completion of his academic programme that was ahead. The courage to continue and complete university, was first and foremost in his mind.

Immediately I constructed a suitable recording environment to fulfill the necessary mechanical requirements, conducive to producing an acceptable audio reproduction of his University texts. The reading transcription process for me was exhilarating. I devoted many hours to the task. In summary, I probably recorded six textbooks for him. It was undoubtedly a mutual learning experience.

Upon completion of his university studies, he pursued a fulfilling career, counselling recently unemployed business personnel, enabling them to modify and adapt their learned skills toward the difficult transition into the workforce. His steadfast determination to proceed under such daunting circumstances, is admirable.

Subordinating myself to a lower level of importance, I wondered, would I possess a similar constitution? These folks have little time for self-pity and bluster. Liberated from an eternal world of darkness, their naked passion for life is exemplary.

I struggled to grasp the undeniable reality of the circumstances surrounding those in attendance. Immersed in their individual nonvisual world, blanketed with darkness, deprived of the influence of physical observation that I have come to expect, on demand.

Instantly, images are dispatched to our brain. Passing through the transparent protective corneal covering, they zoom through the pupil in the middle of the iris, regulating the precise amount of light that enters the eye. The malleable lens focuses the incoming light onto the retina. Photoreceptors produce a high-resolution image, converting it to an electrical impulse which travels along the optic nerve visual pathway, to the brain. The visual image is interpreted.

This complex suite of stimuli - a miracle in itself - responds to my yearning at warp speed, flawlessly. A profusion of vibrant colours, textures, dimension, at my disposal, in a blink of an eye. A mirror image of myself, allowing for self-examination and critique. Ascertaining non- verbal physical responses from friends and acquaintances. Dynamic visuals mesh with a cognitive framework, prompting an awareness and personal belief of my world.

Deprived of vision would surely challenge our ability to overcome a potential onslaught of uncertainty and defeat. The palpable urge to surrender, must be overwhelming. Having personally experienced pterygium removal from my cornea, - surgically excising a benign growth from the surface of my eye- and a life long battle with keratoconjunctivitis -dry eye syndrome- and it's debilitating complications, I do not take my vision for granted.

My learned experience with everyone, illuminated the solidarity that existed amongst themselves. An expressed indication of a sincere comradeship was evident. The group, and others, communicated with an unabashed honesty, from their perspective, the way they see it. Overcoming fear and apprehension. And internally possessing a compulsion to succeed with a personal support mechanism working in harmony with intentional fortitude.

The loss of eyesight does not translate into loss of insight.

6
THE GIFT
BY SHARON SMITH

My son participated in Scouts when he was younger and has learned everything from how to build a fire, to how to help those in our community.

To say that I'm proud of him would be an understatement, but there was one specific time I remember that caused my chest to swell and my heart to burst.

We have an elderly next door neighbour, Victoria, who has been widowed for the past few years. Her husband passed around give years ago and he was the active one in the relationship regarding yardwork as she's confined to a wheelchair and has been since we've known her.

One evening, there was an awful thunderstorm that caused power outages along our street and a lot of chaos with downed trees and other debris. When we woke up the next morning, my son noticed that Victoria's yard had been hit particularly hard. Branches were strewn across the grass, a few things that were on her porch were now on the front lawn, and broken glass from her yard gnome was all over the driveway. It was a mess to say the least.

"Mom, I've got to do something to help Ms. Victoria," my son lamented as I whipped up some batter for pancakes.

"What do you think you can do to help?" I asked.

"Well, I can start by picking up the branches and go from there. I think I'll wait to have breakfast until after I'm finished."

"Are you sure?" I asked. "I know that pancakes are your favourite!"

"Yes, I'm sure," he answered. And with that he bounded down the porch steps into the garage to fetch his tools.

I smiled to myself and at his sense of duty and compassion. I watched from the window as he put the branches into a pile, raked the debris from the lawn, and carefully swept up the glass and put it into a bucket.

Then he knocked on Victoria's door. I couldn't hear what he said, but I watched in silence as he ran back to our house, grabbed two plates and the stack of pancakes that were waiting for him, and went back to Victoria's.

The two of them sat on the porch and chatted as they

shared breakfast.

A couple of days later, I saw Victoria outside on her driveway.

"Your son is an angel," she beamed. "He's such a nice young man and I appreciate his help. You make great pancakes by the way."

I smiled, "He sure is. He's a good boy and turning out to be a fine young man."

"Please let me pay him for his hard work, I tried to give him some money, but he refused," She said as she handed me a crisp twenty-dollar bill.

I shook my head, "He wouldn't let me do that. If I took your money, he'd be right back at your place returning it this afternoon!" I laughed.

"Well, I will find a way to repay his kindness," Victoria said.

Later that year, Victoria passed away. My son was devastated and emotional over the loss of his friend.

Victoria *did* find a way to repay him, I suppose it was something on her heart that she needed to do to show him how much he was appreciated.

I opened the letter and gasped, it was from Victoria's attorney. She had paid for his first year of college in trust.

My son and I cried for a long time after reading the letter from the lawyer, and the last letter Victoria wrote to him.

"The world is a better place because you're in it. Keep doing wonderful things, keep spreading kindness, and continue to do good. We need people like you now more than ever. Thank you for being a friend, to a lonely old lady."

7
WREN RESCUE
BY JOANNE KILKENNY

On a sunny afternoon in July, I took a cup of tea to sit on the deck and enjoy the beautiful afternoon. A short while later, I noticed our dog Lily standing by the edge of the pool looking at something inside. I presumed it was a leaf but got up to see what it was anyway. As I looked down on the stair of the pool, I saw a poor little wren flapping it wings desperately trying to get out. I went to the pool shed to get the skimmer and scoop it out, but as I returned it was floating down the pool heading straight towards the pool filter! I didn't have much time; I dropped the skimmer my mind racing to think of what I could use to save this poor bird!

I ran into the house, pulled open the utensil drawer trying to think what could work best to scoop the bird out without having to touch it with human hands. I spotted the soup ladle, grabbed it, and hurried out hoping I was not too late to save it! The bird was nowhere in sight! I knelt by the pool filter and opened the lid preparing for the worst. I was relieved to see the bird's head still bobbing above the water, trying to fight the pull of gravity into the filter. It looked at me with such terror, not knowing which posed more danger, fighting the force of the water or the human peering down at it.

"Don't worry little one, I am here to help you" I said calmly.

I took the ladle and scooped the little wren out and placed him on the cement. The poor thing was so wet and exhausted, it just collapsed. Not wanting to cause it any more trauma, I walked away and sat on the deck to observe, hoping it would shake its wings and show signs of life.

A few minutes later, three wrens flew in and landed around the poor wet bird. It resembled a rescue team and reminded me of a scene in the movie, The Santa Claus where the elves flew in to rescue Santa. One by one each wren nudged the lifeless bird gently and chirped at it. This went on for some time, each time they waited patiently for it to react. After a while, the lifeless bird seemed to stir, and they continued nudging it ever so gently. The wren shook its wings and tried to stand on its feet but fell back to the ground. With a little more encouragement from the other wrens, it tried again, this time it was successful, stayed on its feet. After it seemed to get its balance, the wrens concentrated on nudging and guiding it to a more protected area under some bushes so it could have time to recover. As I watched the scene, thoughts crossed my mind; I wondered how the wrens knew that one of their own was in need? Had they been in the trees watching my efforts to save the wren? What was it they were communicating to the wren with their chirping? It was a wonderful feeling watching this scene and I felt like I had witnessed a miracle of life.

My husband came out on the deck to observe these feathered friends, taking care of each other just as we humans would. Over the next thirty minutes or so we watched the wrens direct the bird around the pool to the garden area and once it found a safe place which would provide it with visible protection from predators, they flew up in the tree and continued to watch over it.

We decided to head in for dinner, happy that the wren was recovering and waiting for its wings to dry before trying to take flight. I checked on the little wren a few times that evening and watched the yard for any stray animals which could harm it.

Just before dark, I went out one last time and was so delighted that the wren, along with the rescue team had gone on their way before nightfall.

It is hard to describe the emotion I experienced, perhaps awe or sense of wonderment, but it is one that I will not soon forget! It is so rare that humans have the opportunity to observe such a special moment in nature and I was so grateful to have been able to observe and participate in this act of kindness; happy to have saved a little wren's life!

8
ANNE
BY LACEY L. BAKKER

I often run the escarpment trail near my house and during the early mornings, I see the same group of familiar faces. There are women with strollers, dads with dogs, and couples walking hand in hand taking in the sights and sounds on the path above the city. And there was Anne.

Anne was a fixture on the path, she never missed a day of exercise and could always be seen with a huge grin and hand weights as she walked at an unbelievable pace. We'd smile at each other and head in different directions, but this was the extent of our interaction…until the next morning.

It was especially bitter outside as the wind whipped my face and pushed me backward as I tried my best to fight against it. It was a battle, but I was making progress no matter how little.

The snow was falling, and the trail was unusually bare, hardly anyone was out in the blustery weather, but there, like clockwork was Anne.

"Good morning!" She breathed.

The woman was a ray of sunshine and optimism radiated from her.

"Good morning," I said. "I guess it's just you and I this morning!"

"Yep! I admire your tenacity," she said with a chuckle.

"I could say the same about you!"

"I'm Anne, it's nice to finally meet you. I see you out here all the time, but I never give myself a chance to make introductions."

"Lacey, nice to meet you too."

Over the next few blocks, we chatted, and she shared with me that her husband used to come with her each morning until his passing last fall. She kept up her fitness regime as a tribute to him and said that she could feel him watching over her.

"That's really special, I'm sure that he is," I said as we eventually came to the end of the trail which led us our separate ways, "Keep up the good work and I'll see you again soon!"

"Wait, I have something for you," she said. She reached into her pocket and placed a painted stone into the palm of my mitten.

"Use this as a reminder on the tough days like this one; remember that you can do anything!" she said as she bounced away in the other direction, headed back to her home.

I looked down at red pebble and flipped it over. In white writing it said, *You rock!* I smiled to myself and finished my run.

Sadly, I haven't seen Anne since. I wonder what happened to her, maybe she moved, maybe she changed jobs, maybe she didn't walk the trail anymore for whatever reason. I think about her a lot.

The rock she gave me sits on my dresser. I slip it into my pocket every time I go for a run. It's a reminder of the kindness, optimism, and energy that surrounds us, and that I can do anything, even on the tough days.

9

THREE
BY TONYA CARTMELL

Sometimes, it is the small acts of kindness that can have a big impact. Bigger than even those that performed the acts are aware or imagined. Three acts have personally touched my heart and stood out to me during this time.

I live in a small town outside of Hamilton. It is a town where parents play hockey and basketball in the streets with their own children and other neighbourhood kids; neighbours gather to talk or help each other out, and people always smile and say, *Hello*. The town decorates for all the holidays, holds colouring contests, festivals, and movie in the park events. There is a great sense of community here.

When everything started to change in March and families found themselves at home with their children; thoughts turned to what could be done as a community to make this time more fun for the kids stuck at home.

A community Facebook page posted a list of things that people could put up in their windows each week for the months of March and April. That way, parents could take their kids for walks and look for them, almost like a neighbourhood scavenger hunt. It was so much fun to search for, colour, and put up pictures of silly faces, animals, encouraging words, flowers, and Easter Eggs. The neighbourhood was very colourful as you walked around and saw the pictures and inspirational words people had put up in their windows and on their lawns. Some even used chalk to decorate the sidewalk and others painted rocks which they left around town for others to find.

Even though our children are grown, I loved participating in this. Seeing how others had tried to brighten the days of children who could no longer be in school or out playing with their friends, always brought a smile to my face. People also went outside at 7:30 each night to honk their horns or cheer for all the shift workers returning home. Even though my position was moved to working remotely, as a registered nurse, it warmed my heart to do this and see the community acknowledging and celebrating those that were working to care for, and support others in these uncertain times.

Working from home, has been a usual but necessary change for many of us, myself included. For me, working in a fast paced, busy area changed to working from a small desk nestled between the living room couch and the kitchen breakfast bar in my home and interacting with others through Zoom meetings. The conversations with friends over lunch or while running to grab a tea are now a thing of the past.

While my personality leans more to being an introvert, after about five weeks of working from home and social isolating, I was really missing my family and my friends from both my personal and professional lives. Even communication over Zoom for work was mostly done with only audio as many people did not have web cams for their work laptops. While it is still a form of communication, it still lacks the face to face interaction. The people you work with, are the people you spend much of the day with five days a week. They become friends as well as teammates.

I am lucky to work with someone that I have known and worked with for the past eleven years. She is not only a co-worker but someone I also consider to be a friend. Through the years, we have shared a lot of laughter, a few tears, stories of our children growing up, changing organizations to start new jobs, and planning a few fun work events. While our roles no longer had us working together in the same office, we did still check in on each other to catch up.

One day in April, I received a beautiful hand-crafted envelope and note in the mail.

The envelope was made from thick pink striped

cardstock. My address was hand printed onto a small cream coloured post card that was attached with decorative tape. There were flowers and a bird sticker in the bottom left-hand corner along with a "happy day" label. The postage stamp had inked leaves and the saying *This is the beginning of anything you want* on it. The envelope flap was secured by a flat handmade pinwheel decoration.

The notecard inside was made from thick pink and white striped paper. The front had black, white, and green leaves pasted on it, which were overlaid at the bottom with a half circle of white lace that contained a black and white patterned half circle inside of it. There were light green rhinestones around the outside of that with the words, *I am blessed* cut from letters and raised to stand out.

There was a thoughtful handwritten note on the other side. What brought tears to my eyes, was the fact that my friend, who was also dealing with working from home, with her husband and kids who were home from school took the time to create something to send to me. It truly brightened my day to know that someone was thinking of me. It also inspired me to send out post cards to others to let them know I was thinking of them.

I keep the envelope and note beside my computer to remind me that even though our work life may have changed, we are all still connected. It also reminds me to be thankful for the many blessings in my life.

The final random act of kindness occurred in front of my home. My husband and I have an in-law suite for my parents and we also have my sister-in-law living with us. One day we were all outside the front of the house. My mom, sister-in-law and I were looking at the gardens, when a young girl came to the end of our driveway and asked if she could give us a plant. After we talked with her for a few minutes from a safe distance, she left us a beautiful pink flowering plant at the bottom of our driveway.

When we talked to some of our neighbours, we found out that she had left them on other people's porches and driveway all around our neighbourhood. She brightened many people's day with her kind act. My mom followed her example and delivered some plants to people herself.

The plant we received is growing very well in our garden. The bright pink flowers are a reminder to take time and think of others; to share a smile and some kind words.

Small random acts of kindness can be like ripples on the water. You never know how far they will extend or the impact they will make on someone else's life.

10
CURB YOUR ENTHUSIASM (A COVID
MANIFESTO)
BY JOEY NOBLEMAN

One of the benefits of extended COVID-19 home time is
catching up on television viewing and Seinfeld creator
Larry David's current series is especially rewarding. I
have always admired David's art, how he incorporates
and spins the trivial and familiar into amusing, highly
crafted narratives.

Proceeding through the series in the past couple months,
I last night arrived at Season Five's "The Smoking
Jacket", an episode which resonated as I have actually
met three people featured in it. One is director David
Steinberg. Since my youth I have been intrigued by
Steinberg's challenging intellectual, articulate comedy
and diverse talents.

I bumped into Mr. Steinberg a few years ago and our
conversation progressed in a manner you would expect
and hope for as he was not only thoughtful, attentive, and

pleasant but also generous. Understanding that one of my responsibilities was working with high risk youth in a detention centre he penned a detailed note of inspiration for them to be displayed on my Wall Of Fame, an initiative that garnered a considerable degree of notice as it evolved through the years.

Also featured on the Wall of Fame was Richard Kind's pointed message of "Try Harder!" Mr. Kind plays Larry David's cousin Andy. We met in New York City at a special event featuring Sting and Trudy Styler's reading of Robert and Clara Schumann's love letters. Mr. Kind is as animated in person as on the screen, possessing a quick wit and quirky charm. The third personality from "The Smoking Jacket" whom I have met comes not from the world of acting but from professional golf.

The year was 1983, and at age eighteen I had occasion to caddy at the Canadian Open Championship. As a caddy, I had broad access to the facility and one morning, while sitting adjacent to the practice green, I heard the thud-thud of golf balls landing not more than two feet from me, having been dropped there by none other than Jack Nicklaus.

Mr. Nicklaus proceeded to tap a few of them back and forth but was soon interrupted by Gary Player, the golfer featured in David's episode. Mr. Player interrupted Mr. Nicklaus' warm up to introduce his young son whom he had brought to the tournament.

After a brief exchange of pleasantries, Mr. Player parted, proceeding to the driving range and I followed, politely asking if I could watch his exercise. We walked to the far end of the range and I sat on the ground only a few feet from him. He then proceeded, as Bobby Jones said about Jack Nicklaus, to show me a game with which I was not familiar. Each shot traced a Brancusian elegance. I sat quietly, for I was familiar with the story of a woman in a similar circumstance observing Lee Trevino and punctuating each of his swings with a "wow" or "oooh", finally prompting Mr. Trevino's address to her, "Ma'am, I am a professional. What do you expect, ground balls?"

So, Mr. Player and I hung out in quiet trust and mutual respect. So, there we have it, paths crossed with "The Smoking Jacket's" David Steinberg, Richard Kind and Gary Player. My takeaway from that viewing experience is more substantial than just a chance to drop names. What it initially said, or screamed, to me is that the world is small. Or, more precisely, it was yet another reminder that the world is small, and that coming on the heels of the even greater screams that the COVID-19 pandemic recently ushered into my corner of the world. My sally into old television shows was a modest attempt to return to normality.

But before me once again comes the message that the world is so small that we are all connected, a message made all the more curious by its timing, for I recently have been on the verge of certain actions beyond television viewing which have been frowned upon, if not forbidden outright, since the outbreak.

To this time, I have not socialized with friends and family, nor have I attended funerals or celebrations, thus honouring social distancing guidelines. I have sacrificed, not pursuing what I wanted to do regardless of the nobility of the cause. But, admittedly, in the past few days I have been on the verge of succumbing to my selfish desires - and then came "The Smoking Jacket". Meditation on the episode bared even more riches...my meeting with Gary Player was in 1983... with Richard Kind it was during an event hosted by Sting...Sting's Synchronicity was released in 1983...synchronicity...a Jungian concept used as a structuring principle and inspiration for popular art, remarkable.

The synchronicities of "The Smoking Jacket" and my life during COVID-19 are also spinning a narrative, something about the importance of recognizing connections between Day One and Day Today. Therefore, while I wish to gather with others in numbers discouraged by the medical community I will instead remain in sync with their initial and ongoing direction not to. I will also remain in sync with "You Are Not Alone", not in the coddling, nanny-state sense, but with respect to the more salient truth that indiscretion fuels pandemia.

I will synchronize the depth and breadth of my education and experience to take a broad, balanced approach to whatever tries to draw me into the foray. I will take care that my actions reflect well on those who taught me to not do more harm than good in pursuing my causes - I wish my parents to be recognized for doing a good job with me. Thus, I will set aside personal, social, and political agendas until it is safe to externalize them for, as Sting wrote, we share the same biology regardless of ideology.

Throughout, I will resist being swept away by mass fervency, the dangerous madness of which I have had firsthand experience, a tale which I will recount for you…Once upon a time in an educational institution not so far away... a secure facility that housed my country's most dangerous juvenile offenders...where nary a pencil could freely circulate for threat of "shanking"... an elite body - The Committee of Culture (a group composed of one third of the staff) - set about to "normalize" the celebration of Halloween for the residents by having them carve pumpkins with real knives (yes...you read that correctly).

Only a threat of job action clarified for the Committee that neither their facility nor their clientele were normal and the event was mercifully cancelled. That was not a popular outcome, but the moral of the story is that safety and sanity must trump popularity and politics...That experience made tangible to me in short order how "group-think" can spontaneously generate, propagate and sweep away the many, and thus I will instead remain in sync with Thoreau's suggestion that when "do-gooders" come a calling it's best to abruptly head in the other direction.

It also fostered personal reflection, concluding with the uncomfortable acknowledgement that my own IQ and judgement may not be fixed or reliable, but instead fluid, modulating in inverse proportion to the size of any group I am engaged with. I wager that if I, alone, consider handing out knives to those prone to violence I would quickly dismiss it with nervous, embarrassed laughter, as I also would if discussed with one another person.

However, if considered within a group of three, with its altered dynamics driven by the conviction that a group must do something, must act, and other peer and professional pressures discouraging dissent and rationality, I may be compelled to follow. For involvement with groups larger than that, forget about it, there could well be daggers before us. I thus, for myself and for the time being, propose a supplemental slogan - "Continue Remaining Alone".

I also commit to synchrony with Slovoj Zizek's dictate that sometimes the most difficult thing to do, the truly radical act, is to step back, to withdraw, instead of to engage in pseudo activity - another great scourge of our times. Today, stepping back saves lives.

I will thus recommit to fostering thought, discourse and change in manners consistent with, and becoming of, one classically and liberally educated, caringly raised, and imbued with parental wisdom, and having substantial, practical, lived, experience.

Diligent, broad, study; tireless, honest, varied work; positive communal participation and activism; articulate, measured rhetoric in appropriate contexts are the most viable, noble, routes for communication, messaging that, as Sting has put it, reaches a common denominator without it being the lowest. The lowest common denominator of messaging being, say, congregating with thousands during a pandemic.

In essence, I must privilege humans over "humanity", whose categorized abstractions seduce the immature into careless, reckless activity. On maturity, I sync with the Kierkegaardian sentiment that it is achieved by transcending yourself. I will thus understand that my personal agenda is subordinate to the greater good and act accordingly. Unfortunately, one notion I have not been in sync with here is brevity as the soul of wit, and with that recognition I abruptly conclude as follows: when I am next possessed by an impulse to take it to the streets I am simply going to curb my enthusiasm.

11
THE RIVER
BY ALEX GOUBAR

I've lived the same house in southern Ontario since I was two years old. My family emigrated from Belarus when I was five months and was finally able to afford a comfortable townhouse in a neighborhood surrounded by small forests and a system of creeks. We're a family that loves to be surrounded by nature.

One winter afternoon when I was about four or five, my grandmother took me for a walk through the grove by our house. It was chilly but not freezing although it was nearly blizzard conditions. We didn't stray far due to my grandma's bad knee, but she insisted we cross one of the dinky, makeshift log bridges to explore a neighborhood opposite the creek.

To this day I'm not sure if one of the logs were loose, or my clumsy infant self, slipped on some ice nowhere near the bridge, but suddenly I was butt-first in the freezing water. Luckily, the creek was only a foot deep, so being swept away wasn't a danger, although the temperature sure was.

With her help, I managed to climb out of the water. My

grandma was ready with her own coat in her hands to replace my soaking one. She led me back home as I shivered, holding my wet coat in one hand, and my hand in the other, wearing just her sweater.

It was such a silly accident. I felt bad that I ruined our walk, but even worse that she had to endure the cold because of me. I've always appreciated that moment and remember it once in a while; it's not every day you fall into freezing river water.

12
MOO COW
BY KINGA ULAZKA MCDONALD

On July 2, 2020 after an already turbulent, unpredictable, and scary new year, things turned for the worse when my dear cat and love, Moo Cow was attacked by a wild coyote and died.

Moo Cow came to me at a time when I needed him the most. He was a stray on the streets of Mississauga. Some one I knew brought him home to Hamilton. He looked a little ashy grey, was very friendly and he randomly came into our home one day. Gibson fell in love, dexter didn't look like he minded.

We cleaned him up, took him to the vet and began taking care of him. Moo Cow had a terrible bladder infection, so we made sure the vet took care of him well.

He became family. He came in and out of the home, and I hated that he was out doors because of fear he would get hit by a car or taken, it seemed like he was too smart to let anything happen to him. He always kept to the back yards (the homes didn't have fences dividing them) he always came home, and he was big. He took care of himself very well, even though he was scratched up a few times.

We always made sure he was okay. He was a big boy and beyond that, he was the cutest. He had a black mark spilling into his right side and a gorgeous black mark on his left ear. Mostly white, with black marks on his body like a cow, hence why we called him Moo Cow.

He was perfect, we had a morning routine especially when COVID began. I was let off work and we developed a morning, day, and evening routine. He would be let out around 1:00 in the morning, he would be let back in around 6:30am by my husband, he would jump into bed with me, cuddle right on top of me until around 10:00am then treats, more cuddles and love.

Moo Cow is my baby, my love and the rescue that touched my soul.

Moo Cow was the baby I didn't know I needed. He filled me with love, taught me love and always showered me with unconditional loving.

Moo Cow was my baby cow who always graced in the grass out back, followed me on walks with Gibson and always came when I called or shook the treat bag.

Deciding to let go of him was the most difficult decision I ever made. He was clearly in a lot of pain, had a broken leg that couldn't be saved and plenty of internal damage.

He had bite marks all over his body and was severely weak. We could have done surgery, but I couldn't stand the idea of him dying on the table without me. Without love. All alone.

So, we held him, told him he was loved, sang to him, and let him go while we kissed him. It was the hardest thing I ever had to do. Sure, we could of tried doing surgery, but the amount of pain after would not make him comfortable plus the surgery wasn't a guarantee.

I struggle each day and every day. He was my rock, my everything and now he was gone. I needed some comfort and knew the Urn with his ashes would take weeks to get back. I reached out to local painters and asked if anyone was willing to paint him or us together. I received some quotes and of course to uphold his memory my husband and I were willing to do anything, but I was also out of work due to COVID. On top of that we had just spent almost a thousand dollars on trying to save his life.

One artist reached out and said she could do it for free. Her name is Amy Kowalyshyn and some how she knew what I needed. She messaged me and asked if she could do it for free with a new technique she wanted to try. I was overwhelmed with the offer and broke down that day because humanity still existed. I had lost all hope before due to the horrible images all over social media. I didn't think there were good people out there.

In that moment, my grief was too severe for anything to help. I didn't know if anything ever would help. I know this pain will last a lifetime, but in that moment, I realized a stranger cared enough to help with my grief even if it was only for a moment.

During such unpredictable times, something so small meant the world to be because it allowed me to properly preserve my Moo Cow's memory. The cat who brought me back to life and showed me love.

Thank you, Amy Kowalyshyn; you are a light in these dark times.

13
WHEN SHE CRIED FOR THE CRIER
BY ALICIA QUENNELL
(FOR FIONA)

I remember thinking, *we've had a rough go, her and I.*

Cancer. That one is me. Stroke. That one is her.
Challenges at work. Ugh. Honestly, that's definitely both
of us. Special Needs kids. That's both of us too.
However, we've experienced lots of success with our
reading clubs and awesome colleagues through the
Secondary Teacher Library Association (PSSTL), but
lately, just a rough go.

So, I knew turning 40 was going to hit Alicia hard. I
knew this year needed to be something special. I've been
thinking on it for some time because Alicia is someone
who I hold dear to me.

We first met back in 2014 during a library AQ and I
knew immediately we would be friends. She was so
energetic and passionate, an obvious leader. We became

fast friends. In her years as a teacher librarian, she and I made many great memories working together on the Peel Fiction Review Committee as co-chairs, and as Executive Members of the Peel Secondary School Teacher Librarian Association as well.

We also became friends socially, sharing the challenges of raising girls with difficult special needs. After Alicia's injury in 2018 she continued to struggle getting back to work. Then COVID-19 arrived in March and we were all isolated from each other. As Teacher Librarians, we were used to a vibrant, busy, active, collaborative environment; being alone is the opposite to our true nature. Celebrating an important birthday alone would never do.

At the beginning of May I started reaching out to the other members in our library community to make sure everyone was included in my plan and surprise. Alicia would normally host a big bash, but this year things were obviously going to be different. But that didn't mean it would go by quietly. That's not how we roll.

When I found the page for the Town Crier, Andrew Welch, I knew I'd found the perfect way to announce Alicia's 40th birthday this year. I contacted him immediately and set the date. I could barely hide my excitement and of course got on Twitter to leave some hidden clues.

On May 29th, 2020, a young girl's voice called out, "Mommy, someone's here!"

I'd parked just outside her house to be sure I didn't miss her witness the delivery of this message firsthand.

As I waited close by, Alicia stepped onto her porch and said, "Hello good sir. May I help you?"

The Town Crier was dressed in authentic 18th Century regalia. He wore a vibrant red jacket with gold trimmings, reminiscent of British military tradition and history. His regalia was eye catching to say the least!

"Good day m'lady," he began. "Are you, per chance, Alicia?"

"I am," she replied, smiling in her now-small way, and looking around the street.

As he began ringing his golden handbell loudly, a car crept slowly to a halt and the children inside rolled down their windows and leaned out, looking on eagerly.

As the bell ringing continued and his booming voice rang out, several neighbours came out onto their porches to watch. He carefully unrolled his scroll and thus began the epic proclamation of Alicia's 40th birthday announcement.

"Hear ye! Hear ye! Today I am on Diane Drive in the Town of Orangeville! And in particular to those residence of number one-five-two! As an official member of the Ontario Guild of Town Criers, I am here to share news of great joy and celebration! Yay! Let it be known that two score years ago upon this day in the year nineteen hundred and eighty, Alicia Quennell came into this world and therefore today we recognize her fortieth birthday! Though we be in the midst of an ugly pandemic, Birthdays continue, their dates are systemic. This annual event is a fine opportunity to let it be known throughout our community: 'Til we've a vaccine or built herd immunity, fine proclamations can be heard with impunity. The world must embrace the bright side of this virus. The changes, like this, simply serve to inspire us! Happy Birthday Alicia! She's worth a free cry by the company she keeps, like Fiona and all the Peel Library peeps! Proclaimed on this, the twenty ninth day of May in the year 2020, and in the tenth week of pandemic lockdown. Stay safe and well, and may God save the Queen!"

As the street burst into cheers and applause, I drew my attention away from the crier long enough to make eye contact with the birthday girl to see her happy tears while she hugged her girls and blew me a kiss.

The crier continued loudly ringing his handbell and shouted one last time, "Happy birthday, Alicia!"

And I knew for sure it would be a wonderful one.

14
ON BEING SANTA
BY K.G. WATSON

"You were Santa," Sarah said with certainty and the steel-eyed stare of an almost four-year-old.

"I was his helper for today," I admitted. "He's pretty busy these days."

She went back to her hot chocolate, I to my coffee. As the only adult male who regularly stayed through the nursery school classes, I was unusual. Since I wore a full white beard, I was the first choice of the planning committee for the Christmas Party.

They had made their request right after the Hallowe'en party. They'd provide the costume, and a gift for each child purchased by the parent. There would be adult elves to organize the children, hand me the right gift at the right time. I just had to look and sound the part.

"Sure."

Every week when I appeared to give my daughter-in-law the day a week off that I thought any new Mom needed, we went to Nursery school. And every day we went in November, the staff confirmed I was still on for playing Santa. About the end of the month I asked how many children would be at the party. There was always a turnover that made me uncertain what the real enrolment was.

"Twenty-three. Is that a problem?" the organizer asked anxiously.

"No," I replied in my most reassuring voice. I was a retired teacher. "I was just curious."

On my way home, the conviction crystallized that Santa should provide a small token of the day and the party. A bag of triangular cut-offs in my workshop would go to use. They were scraps headed for the garbage at a wood workshop I attended and where I had made a tool caddy. So had many other hobbyists - I had rescued over a hundred pieces. The knot-free wedges would make nice pendants if I could come up with a design.

By the time I returned, the week following, I had settled on a pert reindeer motif. I could use a fine-pointed marker to do eyes and a nose and to write the name and date on the smoothly sanded side of the animal. I could hang it on a bright ribbon. It could be a tree ornament or just a toy box addition or keepsake contribution for Mom's Baby Book, depending on whether the family celebrated Christmas. I had a sample to show the organizer to be sure she approved. From each wedge, I had cut a single figure then sliced it into three clones. They were sanded smooth, had a cheerful smirk, and were an out-of-the-park hit with the Woman in Charge. And better yet, I already had two dozen cut out waiting for the pen details.

Our chat ended with the question, "Did we tell you that the afternoon class will be coming too?"

"No, I wasn't in that loop. How many are in the afternoon class?"

"Twenty," was the reply.

"No problem," I smiled back.

I could make up more tokens that week. I began to mentally organize the shop time to fit into the rest of my other duties.

I was completely prepared when I returned again with a herd of forty-five wooden wafers in the shape of smiling sleigh pullers all standing in slots in an empty chocolate box in the workshop.

"Did someone update you on the change in numbers?" one of the helpers asked as we made ready to leave the class that day.

"Yes, they said the afternoon class would be joining. Forty-three children."

"Yes, that's right and we added the children's siblings as well."

My eyebrows must have popped up, "How many children in total?"

"Seventy-five!"

My brain went into overdrive; two minutes to trace an outline, twenty to cut out, fifteen to split each into three and sand them …

"Well that will be fun," is what I said. "See you next week. Ho Ho Ho."

The workshop went to double shifts that week.

Seventy-five pendants stood side-by-side in ranks in the chocolate box and lid when Santa was about to turn out the light, but his hand hung over the switch. It was all that was required - and more. But … What if someone lost theirs? Or broke it? Or one more child shows up? My hand fell. I turned and went back and cut out two more shapes to make a final six pendants. *I'll hang them on our own tree if necessary,"* I thought.

The church gymnasium overflowed with partywear popping out of snowsuits - princess dresses, small jazzy vests, and bowties. The air crackled with the excitement only children can radiate. Moms were a-twitter with festive greetings and fresh styles. The games, the songs, the stories, went into gear like a machine. No messy artwork today.

"Better get ready," an adult elf suggested, covertly.

The gifting worked out perfectly. Every child got the right gift. Photos to fill a gallery were taken. With the last child stepping back, the chocolate box corral was empty. Whew!

"Everyone loves your pendants, Santa," beamed the organizer. "Do you suppose there might any extra for the women who helped put this on. They would be thrilled."

Wrinkled brow.

"How many," I whispered back.

"Five."

I put on my most serious look.

"Well let's see what's in Santa's magic pocket," I muttered a bit theatrically. My ace wasn't up my sleeve.

With my fingers I counted out what I needed while I did a distraction in my other pocket then back to the first one.

"Well what's this? Ho Ho Ho. Here are ... how many did you need?"

The organizer's eyes were flicking across the collection hanging from my hand. Her smile broke out mixed with relief.

"Exactly five. Thanks Santa."

I was almost to the exit. The helpers were laughing and showing off their pendants when one broke away and hurried to cut me off.

She touched her wooden trinket like it was gold.

"Our leader asked for one for each of us, but she didn't ask for one for herself. You wouldn't happen to have another one…she worked so hard."

My heart leapt but I frowned in dismay.

"Oh my," I said. "Let me see?"

I rummaged again through my roomy coat pockets. One empty hand came out. Another. I tried my trouser pockets. Still nothing. Then back to my jacket and a big smile.

"What's this I find?"

Out came the last pendant carefully wrapped in its ribbon.

She looked at me, suspicious that she'd been played but delighted to see the gift. I don't think anyone noticed my quick steps out the door as soon as she turned back to her group.

Sarah and I were having snacks in the mall hallway later that afternoon. Never take a child home hungry to a parent. A knot of shoppers down the way broke apart to reveal two well-dressed young women marching toward the doorway. Both had bright red ribbons on their necks, just like the one that hung on the child across from me, and they were chatting excitedly, fingering their new jewelry. I couldn't stop laughing and I feel the same way every time that memory returns.

As an adult now, Sarah retells the story each time the reindeer returns.

15
GOING BANANAS
BY P. MARSHALL

It had been a hectic day at work and my mind was scattered all over the place as I got into my car and left to go home. I repeated aloud a list of things that needed to be done before tomorrow morning; put clean laundry away, lay out school clothes for kids, clean rabbit cage, and make lunches. Lunches. I needed to stop for bread, milk, and bananas.

So, I pulled into the grocery store parking lot, got out of the car, and practically ran down the aisles I needed. I waited in line at the register and put my items on the conveyor belt.

I fished around in my purse for my wallet but couldn't find my debit card. *Where in the world was it?* I looked through the pockets, checked my coat, emptied my purse, but my card was no where to be found. My face burned with embarrassment as the line-up grew behind me.

The clerk looked at me and repeated my total.

"I'm sorry, I can't find my debit card. I'll have to put these things back."

Just as I gathered the supplies, a voice behind me spoke up and I turned around to see a mother with her baby.

"It's ok, let me help you out. I'd be happy to pay for your stuff."

"Oh gosh, I couldn't let you do that! Thanks for offering though," I said meekly.

"Please, let me help. I've had a lot of people help me over the years and I want to pay it forward."

I shifted my weight and as much as I felt guilty, I agreed to let her help me.

"Ok, thank you so much. Please give me your address so that I can send you the money to pay for this."

"That won't be necessary, I don't need to be repaid, just pay it forward," she said with a smile.

"Thank you again," I said.

The clerk bagged my groceries and I left with a full heart. I got home, unpacked the food, and searched high and low for my debit card. I found it on the stairs; I had forgotten to put it back into my wallet after paying for a school activity online.

Lunches were packed, laundry was put away, and the

kids were asleep. I put on the kettle and flipped through Facebook to see what my friends were up to. A fundraiser popped up on my feed for a little dog that had been rescued from a horrible situation at a puppy mill. The goal was to raise enough money for the pup to have a surgery that she so desperately needed. The fundraiser was one hundred dollars away from reaching their goal.

I dug out my debit card and keyed in the numbers. I donated the full hundred dollars. When the fundraiser asked me to put down my name, I typed, *The Woman who paid for my groceries.*

I had paid it forward. Just like she asked.

16
GOD BLESS OUR VETERANS
BY MICHAEL JONES

I live in the United States and where I'm from, we have a lot of veterans.

My wife and I were out to breakfast one morning at a local place that we enjoy frequently. It was a rainy day and a bit gloomy. We sipped our coffee and chatted as we chose what to eat. I don't know why I bother to look at the menu since I order the exact same thing each time; eggs (sunny side up), hash browns, two sausage links, and a side of sourdough.

The waitress scribbled down our orders and hurried to put our orders in as more customers poured through the doors.

I noticed that there were a group of older gents that came in together; a few were wearing WWII Veteran caps and one man was wearing a shirt that read, *I'm a Veteran, I fear only God and my wife. You are neither.* I smiled and watched the men for a while until our breakfast came.

My wife and I finished our meals, and I knew what we needed to do. As the waitress came with our check, I asked that the Veteran's meals were added to our bill.

"Are you sure?" The young lady asked.

"Positive." I said as I reached for my wallet.

"Alright, I'll let them know you've paid for them," she said with a grin.

"No. If you could keep this between us, I'd prefer it," I said.

"You betcha," she winked.

I'll never know what it's like to fight in a war because those men fought for my freedom. They are the reason why we are The Land of the Free and The Home of the Brave.

17
THE CHORUS MASTER
BY KEN WATSON

My call to audition was on Saturday morning. It was so bright outside you could see nothing in the darkened sanctuary. Thank goodness for the pool of light around the piano.

"We're ready Mr. Watson," came a voice from the darkness.

The Hymnary I handed the pianist raised an eyebrow. People wanting to join an Opera Chorus bring classical music. I knew none.

The accompanist opened the book at the marker and improvised a heroic rendering of the last line as an introduction.

"Guide me O thou Great Jehovah, Pilgrim through this barren land, I am weak but though art Mighty …" I sang full out, enjoying the reverb that came back from the cavernous space. I was smiling before I got to the last line.

The accompanist provided all the tenor parts that were counterpoint to my bass line in the chorus and then put in a wonderful interlude between the verses.

"Open now the crystal fountain, whence thy healing stream doth flow ... I belted out, looking forward to the decorated tenor addition that came in right on time. My anxiety was melting a bit. Maybe this was fun!

And then we were into the next interlude. I was drawing breath. "Lord, I trust ..."

"NO, Mr. Watson," boomed the voice from the darkness. "We don't need to hear the *third* verse!"

The pianist stopped instantly. The reverb made sure I got it if I'd missed the directive the first time. I didn't know what to do. The plan was to sing, not what to do after. I looked over at the accompanist who was already holding out my music and pointing the way out. I think I crawled through the pile of the carpet to get to the doorway.

A gorgeous soprano voice from the next singer followed me out the door. What a fool I had made of myself to imagine I could join people like that.

I put on a brave face when I got home, and my wife asked how it went.

"Awful," I said.

The kids caught the timbre of my voice. They didn't ask.

I was composing my explanation to my seat mate at the
Welsh Male Voice Choir for Monday night. It was he
who was already in the Chorus and who had suggested I
try out - even that I take a hymn book.

"You sing in the church choir, don't you?"

It would be hard to admit I was not good enough.

*

The pair who had been in the church listening to all those
wanna-be's were the Maestro and the Chorus Master.
The Maestro spoke for them both in declaring that they
had heard enough from me. The Maestro called for the
next singer. The chorus master jotted notes on his sheet
before the soprano started.

There was no time to dwell on spilt milk. I was a
Science Department Head at the local High School and I
had lessons to prepare, experiments to test out to fit in a
forty-minute period. I had tests to mark and there was a
Departmental Budget to start to prepare. I usually didn't
get home before five any school night, but on the Friday
after my audition, I was putting my bike in the shed at
four-thirty. My wife met me at the door.

"They called back," she said handing me the note
with the phone number and 'OPERA HAMILTON', in
block letters across the top. "He said he'd be there till
five."

I only remember fragments of that conversation.

"Thank you for you audition last week," the Chorus Master said smoothly. "We think you have a voice that would develop in our Company and we'd like you to join us …"
I remember writing the date, place, and time.

"We have a Chorus Development Program that we'd recommend you attend …," I think he said.

I wrote down more dates and places and times. I … WAS … IN - well provisionally.   In that moment, I decided I'd walk on live coals before I'd disappoint the Chorus Master's confidence. His name was Peter Oleskevitch.

What Peter did in that decision, was one of the kindest things anyone ever did for me. His invitation enriched my life in that moment and ever after. It started with some pretty heavy-duty time commitments to learn music, and words in many languages, lots of rehearsals; I guessed it took about two hundred hours over a space of less than eight weeks for me to master my part of each production. All that was on top of the chorus development - vocal training, solo prep to present at each group lesson, how to occupy space on stage, body language to broadcast, how to speak four other languages. It was demanding and it was thrilling - like WOW! All that happened because Peter was kind to a musical nonudnick.

Well that's how I felt as I worked my way into the system. I'd taken piano lessons as a child; I'd sung in amateur choirs. Peter had recognized the '*beauty of the untrained voice*' and offered me the chance to train it. I'd never sing a lead role. My place would be in the back row singing the bottom line, but every time I stepped out of the wings into the stage lights, I was helping to make something greater than I could ever be by myself. That was the gift I received, and it was one not given to many.

I sang in over seventy-five productions in the thirty years that followed. I still take pleasure in identifying classical music pieces from the first three notes. How does the brain do that? It is like living in a miracle. We were paid an honorarium at the Opera; it covered your parking, a ticket for your spouse and a cast T-shirt. I tried to bank my money and cover the expenses out of pocket.

The Opera experience and my improving confidence got me invited into an a cappella Carol singing group at Christmas and those were paying gigs also. When I was invited back, I guessed I had passed that audition. I tucked that money away too. The nest egg allowed me to think of being author.

Of course, you had to pass a written audition to be a writer. My publisher copied the kindness of the Chorus Master when she said she'd never been a fan of historical fiction until she read what I'd given her. But she had to follow up her enthusiasm with a practical reality - just like the guidance of the Master so long ago.

"But Watson, you can't punctuate worth beans!"

I had to take lessons.

There is just no end to the effects of acts of kindness. I'm the proof if you need any. It is within everyone's hands to be generous, gracious, kind, a dozen times a day. However small, those acts might be to you, you cannot know the impact and distant consequences they can have.

I've taken to passing out gold stars to those whose diligent efforts are often ignored. When someone has stepped outside their comfort zone to help, when they did so at some cost, when they went past expectation or requirement, I take one from my wallet and put it on the back of their hand in recognition. I've done it all over the world. It is a universal communication of exceptionality. It brightens any day. And you never know where it will lead. It is because of the kindness others have shown me, that I do that to honour their gifts to me.

18
RING FINGER
BY JUSTINE LECHANCE

"Yes! Of course, I'll marry you!" I said to my fiancée as he slipped a gorgeous diamond ring onto my finger.

I hugged him, cried, and immediately got on the phone to text my girlfriends to let them know the good news.

"We have to go out and celebrate! Are you free on Friday night to go out for drinks?" My childhood best friend asked.

"Yes, I'm free!"

"Ok, let's go out for dinner and some drinks. I'll set it up and let you know the details and who's coming."

"Sounds great!" I said as I hung up the phone.

Friday came and I was so excited to meet up with my friends and tell them the story of how Steve proposed. We met at the restaurant and chatted as we placed our orders. Everyone wanted to see the ring and I was proud to show it off.

After a beautiful meal and evening of conversation we changed pace and hit up a local bar for some additional fun. It was so loud and crazy, and people were constantly buying me drinks when they found out that I was engaged.

I went to the bathroom to wash my hands because the daquiri I got was so full it spilled over the top of the glass and created a sticky mess.

I stood at the sink, removed my ring, placed it on the counter and washed the sugar off my hands. Just then a group of girls came into the bathroom hooting and hollering and asked if I had an extra hair elastic.

"No, sorry! I wish! I'd be putting my hair up in a ponytail too if I had one," I smiled and pushed my way through the bathroom door and back out to the dance floor.

As I returned to my friends, I felt a tap on the shoulder.

"I think you forgot this."

I turned around to see one of the girls from the bathroom with her hand outstretched, my ring in the middle of her palm.

My stomach dropped and I burst into tears. How could I have been so irresponsible? I had the ring for less than a week and I had almost lost it!

"Oh my gosh, thank you so much! Thank you so much!" I said through tears as I hugged her.

She patted my back and said, "I'd know how I would feel if I lost my ring," as she held up her finger.

"I can't thank you enough!" I sobbed.

She chuckled and said, "No thanks necessary, but maybe don't tell your fiancée about this for a few years!"

19
THE GAME
BY FRANK LEMON

My son was diagnosed with Autism at the age of three. I was a single dad, and I didn't know what this label meant. I learned quickly that it meant that my son was an almost genius when it came to math, numbers, and memorizing statistics. It meant that he was loving, and kind, and thoughtful, but he wanted to give and get affection on his own terms. It meant that we had appointments with various specialists in speech and other areas of development and it meant that he could have a tough time fitting in with the kids at school from a social aspect.

As Gabriel grew, so did our challenges. He would forget to do his chores because he'd get lost in a computer game. He wouldn't remember to tidy up his room because he was too immersed in a puzzle or was busy reading trivia books.

When we went out to dinner, sometimes people stared at Gabriel and gave him disapproving glances when he interrupted our conversation with something totally off topic and spoke loud enough for others to hear. I knew my son was special and if people only had the chance to see in him what I did, they would love him just as much.

At the age of nine, Gabriel and I moved to a small town near Michigan that was closer to my work. It was the beginning of the summer and I wanted to prep Gabe for the changes that were coming such as a new school and new friends. I laid awake at night praying that he would make friends, just as I had every other year, but my prayers remained unanswered.

Kids just don't understand, I thought. They look at him as odd, but he's the same, just in a different way. A difference in abilities that's all. If only someone would give him a chance. The next day as I was unpacking boxes in the garage and moving things into the house, Gabriel was on the front porch reading a book about baseball.

"Dad! Did you know that your odds are 300,00 to 1 to be his by a baseball and injured if you're in the crowd at a MLB game? Did you know that a regulation baseball has 108 stitches and can be used only once a game?"

The facts came fast and furious.

I laughed, "No, I don't know how many people know that Gabe. Maybe just you!"

"We should go and hit some balls at the diamond over there. Wouldn't that be fun? You should take a break and we should go and play baseball. No one else is there, can we go?"

I glanced at my watch. I had been unpacking for well over two hours and Gabe was right, I could use a break.

"Sure thing, let me just find where I put the baseball stuff and we'll head over."

We walked across the street to the small diamond and I hit the mound while Gabriel stood in the batter's box. He had played baseball almost his whole life, never on a team, but always just the two of us. I tried to get him into little league, but the kids on his team and throughout the league didn't understand his challenges.

I picked up the ball and threw it across the plate, it bounced off the backstop and Gabe picked it up.

"Strike one!" I yelled with a smile.

"Come on, dad! Throw me something I can hit, that was high and inside!"

I threw the ball across the plate and he smacked it into the outfield. By the time I had retrieved it, he was across home plate. It was a home run.

"Whoa!" said a boy who was standing amongst a group of other kids Gabe's age.
"Where did you learn how to hit like that?"

Gabriel stopped in his tracks and said nothing.

"He's been playing baseball since he was a little boy!" I said filling the silence.

"Cool. Can he talk?" Another boy asked me.

I smiled, "He can, he's just shy, that's all."

"Can we play with you guys?"

"Gabriel, would that be ok with you?" I asked my son.

He stood there silently, and I wished he would say something, anything to let me know it was ok.

"You're Gabriel? I'm Gabriel too!" the blonde-haired boy smiled.

This made my Gabriel smile.

"Yes, I'm Gabriel. I'm playing baseball with my dad. His name is Frank. Did you know that a baseball has 108 stitches?"

The other Gabriel smiled back, "No I didn't. Did you know that Babe Ruth almost became the Tiger's manager?"

My Gabriel's eyes widened. Not only did they have the same name, but they both shared a love of obscure baseball facts.

"Should we play ball?" I asked as the other kids

cheered and raced toward us.

Gabriel and Gabriel became fast friends and from that day on, they have been inseparable. Even as the years passed, they did pretty much everything together from sleepovers, to camping trips, to family vacations, and of course baseball games, I'm thankful for the kindness of a young boy that made a difference in my son's life.

Two years ago, my Gabriel was taken from me and became an angel that he was named after.

The other Gabriel, who is like a second son to me, still comes to visit. We talk about baseball and about the fun him and my Gabriel had together over the years. We talk about how much we miss him and sometimes the tears turn to laughter when we remember the good days. I tell him how much his kindness meant to me and what it meant to my son. And he tells me that Gabriel was the brother he never had.

To think, it all started with a simple game. A backyard game that knows no boundaries. Where abilities don't matter, but what matters most is inclusion and acceptance. A game where young men forge friendships that last a lifetime and beyond.

"No act of kindness, however small, is ever wasted."

-Aesop

WAYS YOU CAN SPREAD KINDNESS

1) Volunteer your time or resources. Sometimes it only takes a few minutes of your time to make a difference in someone's life.
2) Smile. A little smile can go a long way. Smile at strangers, smile at babies and kids, be the light that the world needs.
3) Check up on friends and neighbours. There are those who are fighting battles we know nothing about.
4) Give sincere compliments.
5) Donate clothing and food or other resources if you're able to.
6) Tip your service workers if you have the means. Let them know that they're doing a great job and that you appreciate them.
7) Support local businesses and friends. They need your kindness more than ever during this exceptionally challenging time.
8) Share feel good stories online. Brighten your timeline, or a friend's email, with positive quotes, stories of kindness and faith in humanity.
9) Leave an encouraging note. Let someone know you're thinking of them and that they are special and loved.
10) Share the stories. Share Acts of Kindness with friends and family, co-workers, neighbours, leave one at a public place for someone to find. They may find comfort and inspiration here. Pass on the kindness found in the pages of this book.

ABOUT THE AUTHORS

1) **S.P. Taylor**- Silvia Taylor is a Hamilton born writer who loves to be lost in thought, with a smile on her face and a whisper of a story on her lips. Her message is to be kind, love hard, and never give up!

2) **Mary Hassell**- Mary Hassell has been a teacher for 25 years. She writes the way she communicated with her students - empathetically and honestly.

3) **Jake Evanoff**- Jake is a children's book author from Hamilton, Ontario. He released his first book in 2019 and launched his publishing company 'Star Ship Press' just one year later.

4) **M.L. Maple**- I enjoy golf, spending time in the sun and travelling with my family.

5) **Dell Gable-** I have enjoyed interpreting life experiences, utilizing audio and print media. Similarities from past occupational experience, transitioning to the present, have been beneficial.

6) **Sharon Smith**- An avid tennis player who is not so quick on her feet anymore. Sharon enjoys baking and singing while she bakes.

7) **Joanne Kilkenny**- Writing a book was not something Joanne had ever thought of doing until her grand fur-baby Carlos inspired her! Her first book, The Adventures of Carlos: Carlos Goes on Vacation was published this year in both English and French.

8) **Lacey L. Bakker**-Loves animals of all kinds, all types of books, continuing her education, and

enjoys spending time with those she loves.

9) **Tonya Cartmell**- Tonya is a wife, mother, nana, and registered nurse, who at the age of 50 followed her dream of becoming an author with her first children's book inspired by her adopted dog. Her love of the mysterious and unusual fuels her imagination and is now finding its way into her writing.

10) **Joey Nobleman**- Joey Nobleman is an award-winning actor, author, broadcaster, educator and musician whose renaissance manner has been profiled across media. Joey is currently developing a YouTube series inspired by Robert Pirsig's Metaphysics of Quality.

11) **Alex Goubar**- Alex Goubar is a Sheridan college graduate with a passion for illustration. When she's not illustrating children's books, she is camping, playing with her cats, and adventuring.

12) **Kinga Ulazka Mcdonald**- Kinga is a Graduate of McMaster University, owns a small floral business in Hamilton, ON and is planning to attend Law school. She adores her fur-babies and hopes to be a published writer

13) **Alicia Quennell**- Alicia is a teacher and mother who finds her inspiration for writing shorty stories, poetry, and fiction from the everyday experiences she has with her family and pets. She lives with her husband and two daughters in Orangeville, ON

14) **K.G. Watson**-Author of five books in print so far, history buff, and all-around captivating storyteller.

15) **P. Marshall**- I like to read stories to my grandkids, talk on the phone to friends, and send letters through the mail like the good old days.

16) **Michael Jones**-I love working on old cars, listening to good music, and riding horses with my wife.

17) **Ken Watson**-Ken enjoys gardening, reading, tracing his family history, and writing. He also enjoys singing and creating a weekly newsletter for friends and family.

18) **Justine LeChance**- I enjoy old movies, romance novels, and getting dressed up to go out with my husband.

19) **Frank Lemon**-Baseball, books, and my boy are my first loves. Not in that order. I also enjoy a good bottle of Scotch, the older the better.

ADDITIONAL BOOKS BY
PANDAMONIUM PUBLISHING HOUSE
CAN BE FOUND IN MAJOR BOOKSTORES, ON
AMAZON AS PAPERBACK AND E-BOOK
VERSIONS, AND ON OUR WEBSITE
WWW.PANDAMONIUMPUBLISHING.COM/SHOP

The funds from the purchase of this book has been paid forward.
We've made a donation to various organizations that are close to our
heart from the proceeds collected.

www.pandamoniumpublishing.com
www.pandamoniumpublishing.com/shop
pandapublishing8@gmail.com